ISIS

QUEEN OF THE EGYPTIAN GODS

by Amie Jane Leavitt

Content Consultant
Rita Lucarelli, PhD
Associate Professor of Egyptology
University of California, Berkeley
Berkeley, CA

CAPSTONE PRESS
a capstone imprint

Snap Books are published by Capstone Press,
1710 Roe Crest Drive, North Mankato, Minnesota 56003
www.capstonepub.com

Library of Congress Cataloging-in-Publication Data
Library of Congress Cataloging-in-Publication data is available on the Library
of Congress website.
ISBN 978-1-5435-7414-2 (library binding)
ISBN 978-1-5435-7554-5 (paperback)
ISBN 978-1-5435-7418-0 (eBook PDF)

Editorial Credits
Michelle Parkin, editor
Bobbie Nuytten, designer
Svetlana Zhurkin, media researcher
Katy LaVigne, production specialist

Image Credits
Alamy: Album, 26, Ivy Close Images, 21, Lanmas, 14, Magica, 13, The
Hollywood Archive/PictureLux, 29 (top); Newscom: Heritage Images/Werner
Forman Archive, 24, Oronoz/Album, 7 (top); Shutterstock: Airijo, 9 (bottom),
Everett Art, 23 (left), Jose Ignacio Soto, cover, 12, Katika, 7 (bottom), kilukilu,
22, Masterrr, 16, Protasov AN, 18, reptiles4all, 25, Sompol, 28, Ttatty, 11,
Vladimir Wrangel, 29 (bottom); SuperStock: Pantheon, 10; The Metropolitan
Museum of Art: Rogers Fund, 1945, 23 (right)

Illustrations by Alessandra Fusi
Design Elements by Shutterstock

All internet sites appearing in back matter were available and accurate when this
book was sent to press.

Printed and bound in the USA.
PA70

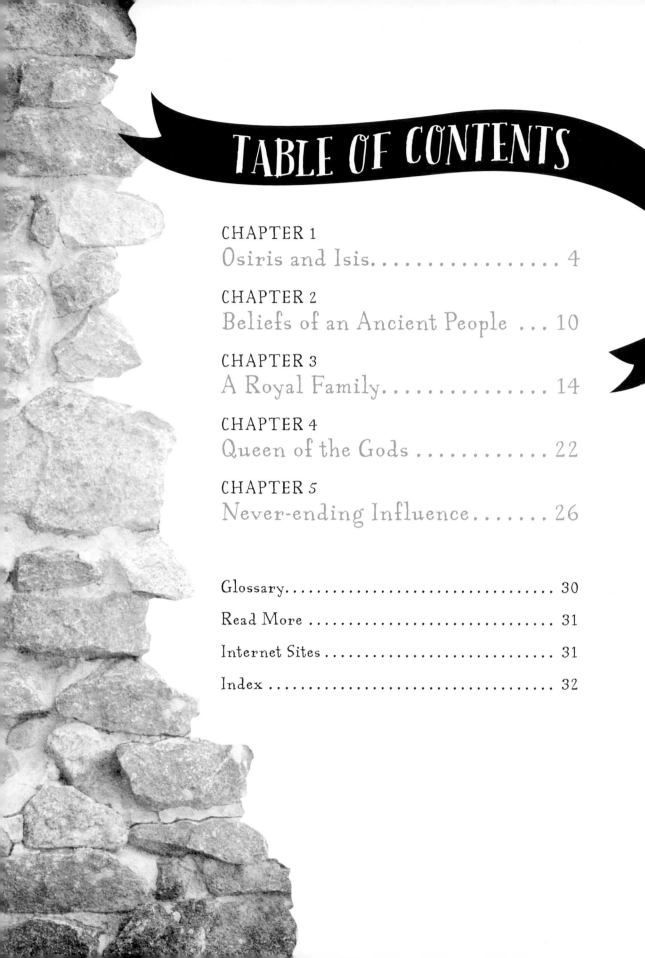

TABLE OF CONTENTS

Chapter 1

OSIRIS AND ISIS

Being one of the gods of Egypt wasn't enough for Seth. He wanted to be king. He wanted what his brother had.

Seth's brother Osiris was the chief god and king of Egypt. The ancient people loved him. Osiris was married to Isis, queen of the Egyptian gods. Seth looked at everything his brother had and shook with rage and jealousy. Seth was determined to take Osiris's place as king—no matter what it took.

One evening Seth hosted a grand party. He invited all of the important people of Egypt, including Osiris. At the party, Seth presented a beautifully decorated wooden box.

"Whoever fits inside this box will keep it forever!" Seth announced.

All of the guests wanted the box for themselves. One by one, they climbed in. No one fit inside. Some were too long, and some were too short. Some were too wide, and some were too thin. The box was not a match for anyone.

Isis and Osiris

Finally it was Osiris's turn. The king gently climbed inside the box and lay down. To everyone's delight, Osiris fit perfectly inside. There was even room for the lavish crown on his head. It was obvious. The box belonged to him.

Seth smiled with a sinister grin. This was his plan all along. As soon as Osiris was comfortably inside, Seth slammed the box's lid and locked it. Osiris couldn't escape. The box had become Osiris's coffin.

"As promised this box is yours forever, Osiris," Seth cried as he pushed Osiris and the box into the Nile River. "Now I can take my rightful place on the throne!"

The news spread throughout the kingdom. Osiris was gone. Seth was the new king of Egypt. The people were devastated. But no one took the news harder than Isis. Osiris's beloved wife missed him terribly. She spent her days mourning her great loss. Weeks passed. Finally, the goddess made a decision—she had to have Osiris back. If she could find the box, she could use her magical powers to bring him back to life.

Isis searched for the wooden box in every corner of the kingdom. Eventually she found it in the faraway land of Byblos. She was able to convince the people who lived there to give it to her.

Isis came home to Egypt with Osiris's body. But before she could bring Osiris back to life, Seth found out about his return. Seth did not want to give up his throne. He rushed to where Isis had stored the box and unlocked the lid. Then Seth chopped Osiris up into 14 pieces. He threw the pieces all over Egypt.

Isis found out what Seth had done. But it didn't stop her. Isis was determined to have her husband back. The goddess grew a giant pair of wings and flew from one end of the kingdom to the other. From her view in the sky, Isis found all the parts of Osiris's body—except for one. She made the last piece out of gold.

Carefully, Isis put Osiris back together. Then she covered him with strips of cloth. Osiris had become the first Egyptian mummy. Once his body was wrapped, Isis used powerful magic to bring Osiris back to life.

Osiris opened his eyes. Isis felt a great sense of joy and started to celebrate. Osiris was alive! But the celebration was short-lived. Osiris told his wife that he couldn't stay. Since he wasn't whole, Osiris couldn't rule over Egypt as he used to. Instead, he had to rule the **underworld** as king of the dead.

After Osiris became ruler of the dead, Isis had a baby. She named him Horus. As Osiris's son, Horus was the **heir** to Osiris's throne on Earth. But Isis knew Seth wouldn't give up the throne without a fight. This was a dangerous time for Horus. Isis and her son hid so Seth couldn't find them.

When Horus got older, he challenged his uncle for the throne. A great battle raged. During the fight, Seth poked out Horus's left eye. Eventually Horus defeated his evil uncle. Seth was overthrown and banished from Egypt forever. Peace returned to the land.

Horus (left), Osiris (middle), and Isis (right)

underworld—the place where ancient Egyptians believed the spirits of the dead go

heir—someone who has been or will be left a title or property

GODDESS FACT

Horus's left eye was a powerful symbol of healing in ancient Egyptian culture.

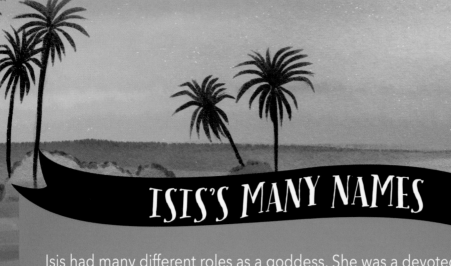

ISIS'S MANY NAMES

Isis had many different roles as a goddess. She was a devoted wife, mourner, magical healer, and protective mother. Isis cured the sick and was a role model for ancient women. She was also responsible for the rites of the dead. These special burial **rituals** were performed to guarantee a person's success in the afterlife. In Egyptian culture, Isis had a different name for each of her roles.

ISIS'S NAME	ROLE
SATIS	flooded the Nile River to give life to the surrounding land
KHUT	giver of light at the beginning of the new year
RENENET	goddess of a successful harvest
AMENT	goddess of the underworld; responsible for restoring the bodies of the dead so they can live with Osiris
TCHEFT	goddess of the food given as offerings to other gods and goddesses
ANKHET	goddess of fertility
THENENET	goddess of the underworld; also known as the Tuat
USERT	goddess of the earth
KEKHET	goddess of the fields

Isis as Renenet, goddess of the harvest

ritual—set of actions or prayers carried out by priests or worshippers

pharaoh—a king in ancient Egypt

descend—to come from the ancestral line of someone who lived a long time ago

····· GODDESS FACT ·····

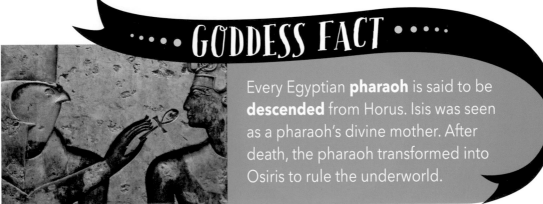

Every Egyptian **pharaoh** is said to be **descended** from Horus. Isis was seen as a pharaoh's divine mother. After death, the pharaoh transformed into Osiris to rule the underworld.

9

Chapter 2

BELIEFS OF AN ANCIENT PEOPLE

Like many groups in the ancient world, the Egyptians created myths to explain what happened around them. These myths often involved gods and goddesses. The people worshipped and prayed to these **deities**, offered **sacrifices**, and paid tribute to them in special temples.

This ancient Egyptian religion began with a myth that explained how the world, sky, and sea were created. The god responsible for all of this was Ra, the creator and sun god. Not only did he make Earth but he also created the other gods. These gods and goddesses were called the Ennead, or *the Nine*. They included Shu, Tefnut, Geb, Nut, Osiris, Isis, Seth, Nephthys, and Horus. The gods Osiris and Isis were the first rulers of Egypt.

Geb, the god of Earth, is often shown lying on the ground. Nut is the sky goddess above him. Shu is the air god between the earth and sky. The other six gods are around them.

An ancient mummy was on display near Cairo, Egypt.

LIFE AFTER DEATH

Ancient Egyptians believed that death was a transition from one state of being to another. Death was not the end but rather a new beginning. If a person's body was intact, the dead could move on and live in the afterlife. To do this, ancient Egyptians **mummified** their dead and placed them in **tombs**. The mummification process was very expensive. Only royalty, officials, and commoners who could afford it were mummified.

deity—a god or goddess

sacrifice—to offer something to a god or goddess

mummify—to preserve a body with special salts and cloth

tomb—a room or building that holds a dead body and any items that were buried with that person

MUMMY MAKING

To make a mummy, priests removed the moisture from the body, including the blood and most of the organs. The heart was left inside. Ancient Egyptians believed that this was the center of the person's spirit. The stomach, liver, lungs, and intestines were placed in separate containers called canopic jars. One of Isis's duties was to watch over the liver canopic jar. The mummy was covered in a special salt to dry out. Then it was wrapped in strips of linen cloth. The mummy could be preserved for centuries because of Egypt's dry conditions.

Inside the tomb, the mummy was placed in a wooden coffin or stone **sarcophagus**. The tomb was filled with items that the person would need in the afterlife. There was food, jewelry, furniture, and statues of gods and goddesses.

There were also **murals** on the walls. These gave instructions about how to enter the afterlife. The murals included spells and images from the *Pyramid Texts* and the *Book of the Dead*.

GODDESS FACT

Archaeologists learn about ancient Egyptians and their way of life by studying mummies.

Pyramid Texts

The *Pyramid Texts* are the oldest known religious writings in the world. They date back to 2400 B.C. Written in **hieroglyphics**, the *Pyramid Texts* contain spells that the pharaohs needed to move on to the afterlife. More than 200 gods and goddesses are mentioned in the *Pyramid Texts*. Isis is mentioned many times.

Pyramid Texts carved on the walls in the pyramid of Teti

sarcophagus—a stone coffin
mural—a wall painting
archaeologist—a scientist who studies how people lived in the past
hieroglyphic—a picture or symbol used in the ancient Egyptian system of writing

Chapter 3

A ROYAL FAMILY

Isis was one of the oldest goddesses in ancient Egypt. She was the daughter of Geb and Nut. Geb was the god of the earth. Nut was the goddess of the sky. They had four children—Osiris, Isis, Seth, and Nephthys.

Isis was close with her sister Nephthys. They both had powers to help the dead. They are often shown together in Egyptian artwork. Isis is both the sister and wife of Osiris. In ancient Egypt, the deities and pharaohs often married their siblings. This ensured a royal bloodline.

In a page from the *Book of the Dead*, Osiris sits on a throne. Isis and Nephthys stand behind him.

THE CHILDREN OF ISIS

Osiris and Isis had a son named Horus, who became ruler of Egypt. Isis also adopted several children. Anubis was the son of her sister Nephthys. Isis raised Anubis as her own. Isis also adopted Imsety, Hapi, Qebeh-Sennuef, and Duamutef. Called the Four Sons of Horus, these gods helped guard the canopic jars in the tombs.

The god Anubis is often shown with the head of a jackal or wild dog.

Isis's Family Tree

TEFNUT

The goddess of rain was Isis's aunt.

SETH

The god of chaos was Isis's brother.

SHU

The god of air was Isis's uncle.

NEPHTHYS

The Egyptian goddess of mourning was Isis's sister.

ISIS

The Egyptian goddess of the sky was Isis's mother.

NUT

GEB

The god of Earth was Isis's father.

The god of the dead was Isis's husband. He was also her brother.

OSIRIS

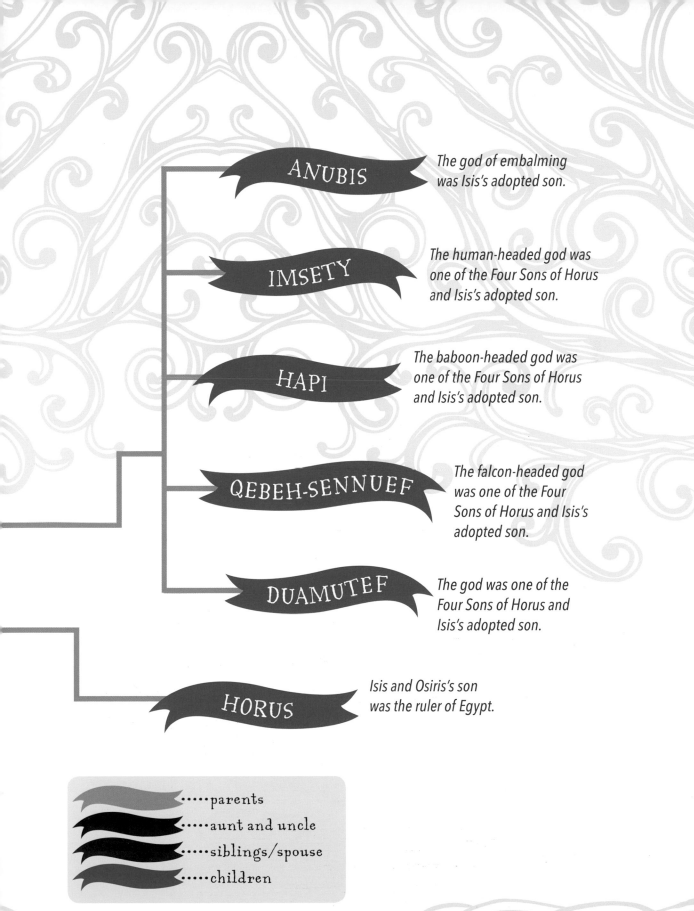

ANUBIS

The god of embalming was Isis's adopted son.

IMSETY

The human-headed god was one of the Four Sons of Horus and Isis's adopted son.

HAPI

The baboon-headed god was one of the Four Sons of Horus and Isis's adopted son.

QEBEH-SENNUEF

The falcon-headed god was one of the Four Sons of Horus and Isis's adopted son.

DUAMUTEF

The god was one of the Four Sons of Horus and Isis's adopted son.

HORUS

Isis and Osiris's son was the ruler of Egypt.

·····parents
·····aunt and uncle
·····siblings/spouse
·····children

ISIS AND THE SEVEN SCORPIONS

When Horus was a young child, he and Isis lived in the swamps near the Nile River. They hid in the tall **papyrus** reeds where Seth couldn't find them. Anytime Isis left the swamp, she traveled with seven powerful scorpions.

One night, it was too late for Isis to return to the swamp. The goddess turned herself into a beggar and looked for a place to stay in a small Egyptian town. A wealthy woman saw Isis as a beggar and shut her door.

"There is no room for you here," the woman yelled out when Isis knocked.

The scorpions were enraged by the woman's behavior. As punishment, they combined their poison. Then one scorpion snuck into the wealthy woman's house and stung her child. The child became deathly ill.

papyrus—a tall water plant that grows in northern Africa and southern Europe

yellow scorpion

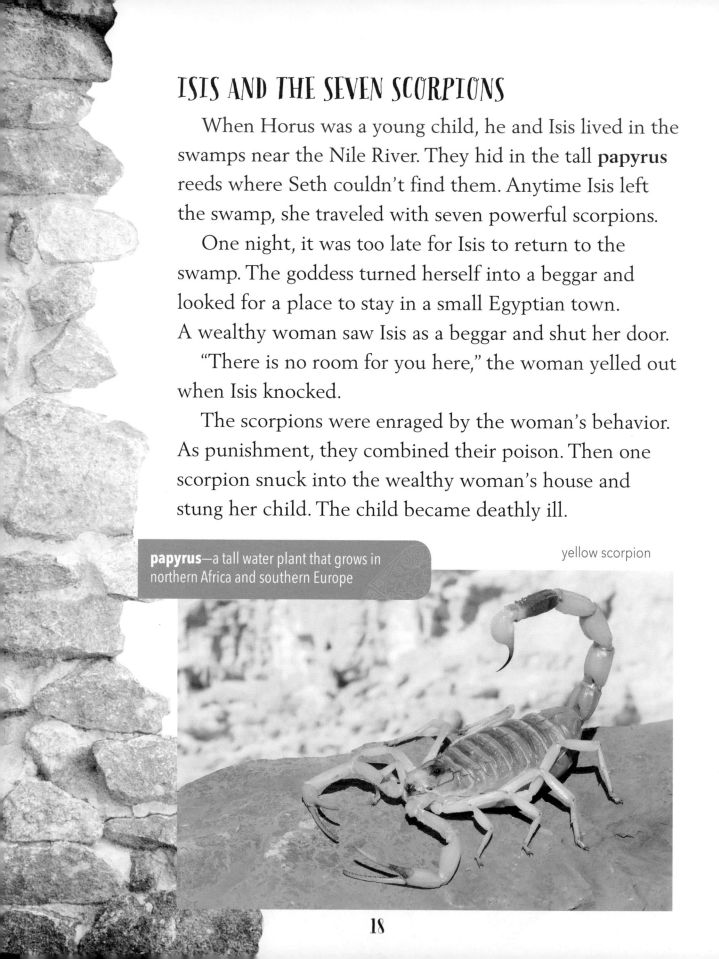

18

"Please, someone help my son!" the woman called through the town.

Isis heard the woman's cries and took pity on her. The goddess hurried to the child. She held him in her arms and whispered a magic spell. The child recovered. The wealthy woman felt shame and regretted how she had treated the goddess. She gave Isis all of her worldly possessions.

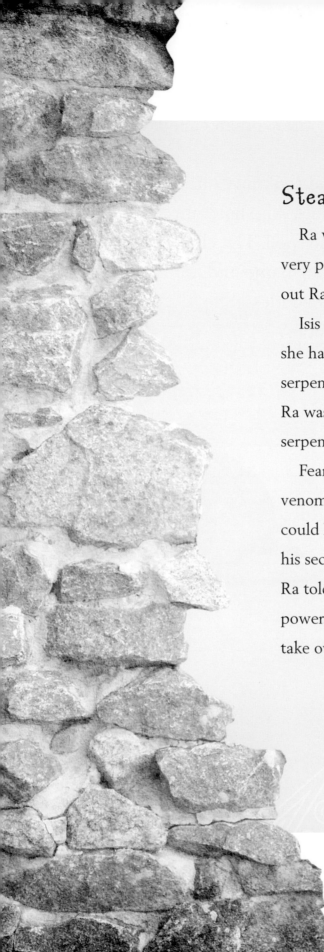

Stealing Ra's Power

Ra was Isis's grandfather. The mighty sun god was very powerful, but he had a secret. If anyone found out Ra's name, he would lose some of his power.

Isis wanted this power for her son, Horus. So she hatched a plan. Isis used her magic to make a serpent. She placed the serpent on the road where Ra was known to walk. When Ra walked by, the serpent bit him.

Fearing that he would die from the snake's venom, Ra called for Isis. He knew that her magic could heal him. Isis agreed to help Ra if he told her his secret name. Ra refused, but Isis insisted. Finally Ra told her his secret. Now Isis had part of Ra's power. She gave the power to Horus, who used it to take over Ra's throne.

Isis (left) and Ra

Chapter 4

QUEEN OF THE GODS

In Egyptian artwork, Isis is shown as a young woman in a long dress. In one hand, she holds a staff of papyrus. This represents her time hiding in the swamps with Horus. She holds an ankh in the other hand. This symbol means life.

In other images, the goddess sits on a throne nursing her baby. She wears a crown that looks like an empty throne. Some believe this represents Osiris's empty throne on Earth. Sometimes Isis wears cow horns, a sun disk, or a crown shaped like a vulture. In other works of art, Isis has eagle wings attached to her back or arms.

Isis with eagle wings

Isis is often depicted as a mother with her baby. Some people believe this inspired images of the Virgin Mary holding baby Jesus.

the Virgin Mary and baby Jesus

Isis and Horus

SPECIAL POWERS

Isis's main power was magic. She could cast spells, raise the dead, and heal the sick. Her powers were greater than all of the other Egyptian deities combined. Isis was considered the chief magician in ancient Egypt.

When people were ill, family members prayed for Isis's help. The goddess protected the dead and helped them enter the afterlife.

Isis offered protection to worshippers.

PERSONALITY AND CHARACTERISTICS

Isis was one of the most beloved goddesses in all of Egypt. She was a good ruler who supported her people. She was seen as persistent and brave in the face of great challenges. She was also a devoted mother who would do anything to protect her children.

Isis was a teacher. She taught the women of ancient Egypt how to grind corn and make bread. She also showed them how to spin **flax**.

····· GODDESS FACT ·····

Isis's **sacred** animals are the cow, snake, and scorpion. She is also the patron goddess of hawks, swallows, doves, and vultures. Sometimes Isis is depicted as one of these animals in Egyptian artwork.

flax—a plant that produces linen for fabrics
sacred—holy or having to do with religion

Chapter 5

NEVER-ENDING INFLUENCE

Many people worshipped Isis, whether they were rich or poor, young or old, or male or female. The ancient Egyptians held special festivals in her honor. One was called the Night of the Teardrop, which was held every year. This festival celebrated the flooding of the Nile. Ancient Egyptians believed this flooding was caused by the goddess's tears after Seth murdered her husband.

GODDESS FACT

Isis was worshipped in Heliopolis, also known as the "City of the Sun" or the "House of Ra." Heliopolis was one of the oldest cities in Egypt. Some believe that the priests of Heliopolis created the Isis myths.

FAR AND WIDE

Egyptians weren't the only ones who prayed to Isis. Her influence can be found in many places throughout the ancient world. The Greeks and Romans both worshipped her. She has often been compared to the goddesses Demeter, Persephone, Tethys, and Athena in Greek mythology. The Romans associated Isis with the goddesses Ceres and Venus.

In ancient Rome, a special festival called Navigium Isidis was held to honor Isis. The Romans believed that Isis controlled the sea. This festival was used to pray for Rome's sailors. People dressed up in costumes and carried a model ship through the streets. Worshippers took the ship from Isis's temple to the sea.

Ancient Romans celebrated Navigium Isidis every March.

Temples to Isis

Since Isis was worshipped in many places in the ancient world, there were numerous temples built in her honor. There were temples in the Egyptian cities of Philae, Behbeit el-Hagar, and Alexandria. Isis was worshipped in Delos, Greece. Temples were also built in Pompeii and Rome in Italy, as well as Ephesus in Turkey. There are even remnants of an Isis temple in London, England. Archaeologists believe it was used around the 500s.

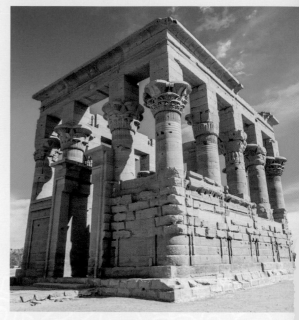

The Temple of Isis was in Philae in Egypt.

ISIS IN POP CULTURE

Isis still impacts popular culture today. Different religions throughout the world still worship the Egyptian queen. In addition, pop culture has used her ancient stories to inspire their characters.

JoAnna Cameron played the goddess in *The Secrets of Isis*.

In the 1970s, a TV show called *The Secrets of Isis* aired on Saturday mornings. In this show, a high school teacher called upon the powers of Isis after discovering an ancient necklace. Isis's powers made the woman incredibly strong. She could fly at super speeds, move objects without touching them, and control the weather. She even acted as a lightning rod during thunderstorms.

A new DC Comics superhero named Adrianna Tomaz was introduced in 2006. She had Isis's powers. A similar character named Zari Adrianna Tomaz is featured on the TV show *Legends of Tomorrow*.

GODDESS FACT

Wolfgang Amadeus Mozart composed the opera *The Magic Flute* in 1791. Some believe he was inspired by myths about Isis.

GLOSSARY

archaeologist (ar-kee-AH-luh-jist)—a scientist who studies how people lived in the past

deity (DEE-uh-tee)—a god or goddess

descend (dee-SEND)—to come from the ancestral line of someone who lived a long time ago

flax (FLAKS)—a plant that produces linen for fabrics

heir (AIR)—someone who has been or will be left a title or property

hieroglyphic (HYE-ruh-glif-ik)—a picture or symbol used in the ancient Egyptian system of writing

mummify (MUH-mih-fy)—to preserve a body with special salts and cloth

mural (MYU-ruhl)—a wall painting

papyrus (puh-PYE-ruhss)—a tall water plant that grows in northern Africa and southern Europe

pharaoh (FAIR-oh)—a king in ancient Egypt

ritual (RICH-oo-uhl)—set of actions or prayers carried out by priests or worshippers

sacred (SAY-krid)—holy or having to do with religion

sacrifice (SAK-ruh-fisse)—to offer something to a god or goddess

sarcophagus (sar-KAH-fuh-guhs)—a stone coffin

tomb (TOOM)—a room or building that holds a dead body and any items that were buried with that person

underworld (UHN-dur-wurld)—the place where ancient Egyptians believed the spirits of the dead go

READ MORE

Braun, Eric. *Egyptian Myths*. Mythology Around the World. North Mankato, MN: Capstone Press, 2018.

Drimmer, Stephanie Warren. *Ancient Egypt*. National Geographic Kids Readers. Washington, D.C.: National Geographic, 2018.

Napoli, Donna Jo. *Treasury of Egyptian Mythology: Classic Stories of Gods, Goddesses, Monsters, and Mortals*. National Geographic Kids. Washington, D.C.: National Geographic, 2013.

INTERNET SITES

Ancient Egyptian Gods and Goddesses.
https://www.ducksters.com/history/ancient_egyptian_gods_goddesses.php

BBC: History for Kids. Ancient History.
http://www.bbc.co.uk/history/forkids/

INDEX